HOW BIG IS BIG?
From Stars to Atoms

By HERMAN and NINA SCHNEIDER
Illustrated by SYMEON SHIMIN

Is there anything bigger than the Empire State building or the Rocky Mountains, or anything smaller than a flea or a mite? And how big are you in relation to the biggest and smallest? In this simple science book, every child can understand that it would take 25 skyscrapers to equal a mountain, but then the moon and the stars and sun are even bigger. And at the other end of the scale are the algae and the atoms. But all children are just the right size—not too big and not too small.

* * * *

Dewey Decimal Classification: 500

HOW BIG IS BIG?

FROM STARS TO ATOMS

By Herman and Nina Schneider

With Illustrations by Symeon Shimin

THIS SPECIAL EDITION IS PUBLISHED BY ARRANGEMENT WITH
THE PUBLISHERS OF THE REGULAR EDITION
WILLIAM R. SCOTT, INC.
BY
E. M. HALE AND COMPANY
EAU CLAIRE, WISCONSIN

Everybody is always telling you how big you are. Your mother says, "Look at your clothes! You're popping out of them."

Your father says, "Yes, you certainly are big now."

You look in the mirror and wonder, "Why do they all say I'm so big? How big is big?"

An elephant is big. He is the biggest animal in the zoo. If you go for a ride on an elephant, the ground looks very far away. High up there on the back of the big elephant he seems to be the biggest thing in all the world.

Is there anything bigger than an elephant?

Most trees are much taller than the biggest elephant. Even if the elephant lifts his trunk way up, he can't reach the top of a tall tree. It would take many elephants standing one on top of the other to reach the top of the tallest tree.

A tree is very big. Is anything bigger than a tree?

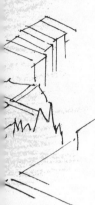

A skyscraper is much bigger than a tree. A tall tree doesn't look very big next to a skyscraper. If you went up to the top of the skyscraper and looked down, the biggest tree would look like a toy tree.

A skyscraper is tall. It is taller than the tallest tree in the world. But is there something bigger than a skyscraper?

A mountain is bigger than a skyscraper. This is how the biggest building in the world would look next to the highest mountain in the world.

Twenty-five skyscrapers, piled one on top of another, would be as high as that mountain. Is anything bigger than the biggest mountain?

The moon is bigger than the biggest mountain. This is how big the mountain would look next to the moon. The huge mountain, which is bigger than a skyscraper, bigger than a tree, bigger than an elephant, is not nearly as big as the moon.

The moon, which looks as if it could hide behind a chimney, seems small only because it is so far away. The moon is very, very big. Is anything bigger than the moon?

The earth that we live on is
bigger than the moon. If you could
fly an airplane around the moon, it
would take you a whole day and
night. It would take you four
whole days and nights to fly
around the earth.

The earth is huge, but is the huge
earth the biggest thing of all?

No. Every clear morning you look out of the window and see something much bigger than the earth. Far, far off in the sky, the huge shining sun is much bigger than the earth. Is there anything still bigger than the sun?

Yes. Some faraway stars that twinkle in the sky are hundreds of times bigger than the sun.

The stars are the biggest things we know.

So many things are bigger than
you are, why do people say you are
so big?

You are smaller than a star,
smaller than the sun,
smaller than the moon,
smaller than the mountain,
smaller than a skyscraper,
smaller than a tree,
smaller than an elephant.

How small *are* you?

How small is small?

A puppy is smaller than you are.
A puppy is small enough to be quite
comfortable sniffing around under
a dining room table. People's legs
look very high to a puppy.

A puppy is small. But is there
something smaller than a puppy?

A mouse is smaller than a puppy. He is too small to pick up even the smallest of the puppy's collection of bones. A little pet mouse is so small that he can sit in your hand.

Is anything smaller than a mouse?

A flea is smaller than a mouse. To a flea the mouse is very big. The flea has to take a long walk to go from one end of the mouse to the other.

Fleas are so small that an ash can will hold more of them than there are people living in the whole United States. But fleas are not too small to learn to act in circuses. They are trained to pull tiny wagons, wheelbarrows, and cannon. Special magnifying glasses are needed to make the tiny fleas look big enough for people to see them act.

Fleas are small. But there are things even smaller than fleas.

A mite is smaller than a flea. A flea is tiny, but he looks very big to the little mite on his back. This little animal can ride on a flea's back as easily as you can ride on an elephant. This is how a mite riding flea-back would look under a very strong magnifying glass. A mite is so small that a blade of grass is a broad highway to him.

A mite is very small. Is there anything still smaller than a mite?

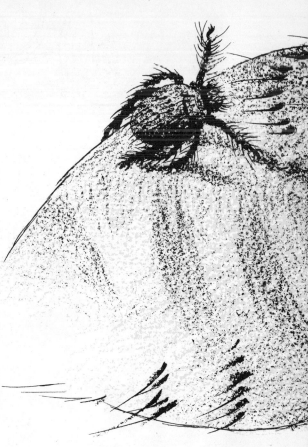

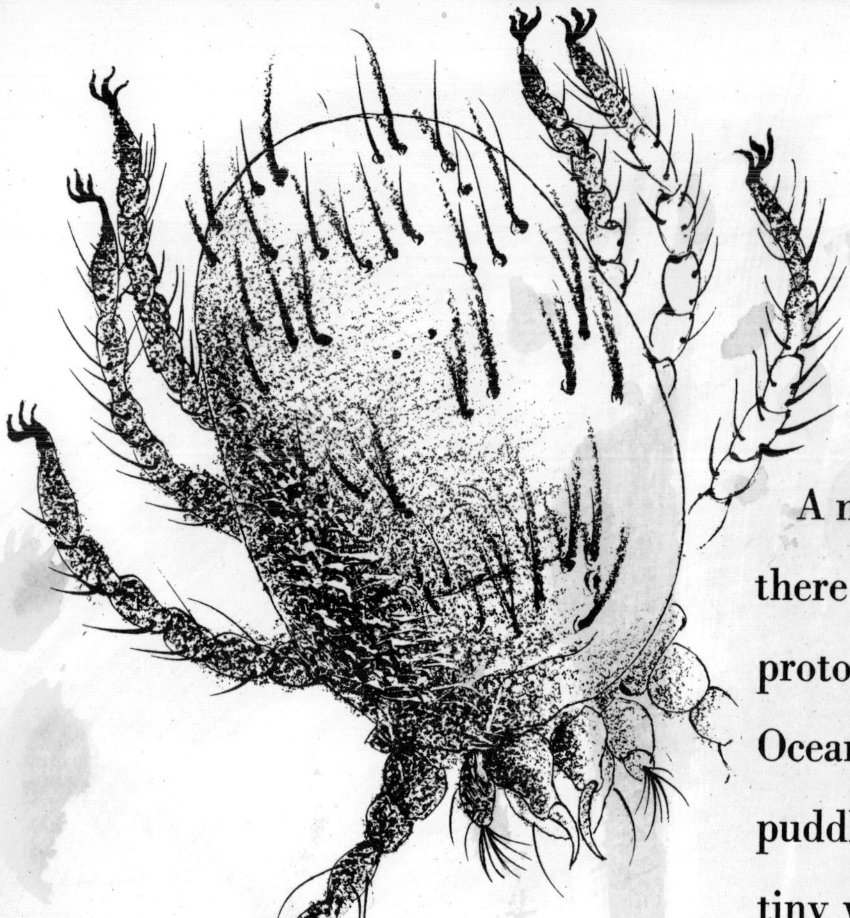

A mite is very small indeed. But there are tiny water animals, called protozoa, that are smaller still. Oceans and lakes, ponds and mud puddles all have some of these tiny water animals in them.

A drop of water from a flower bowl has dozens of kinds of protozoa scurrying around in it. If you look carefully, you can see the larger ones as tiny specks. This picture shows them hundreds of times bigger than they are.

Protozoa are very small, but are they the smallest things of all?

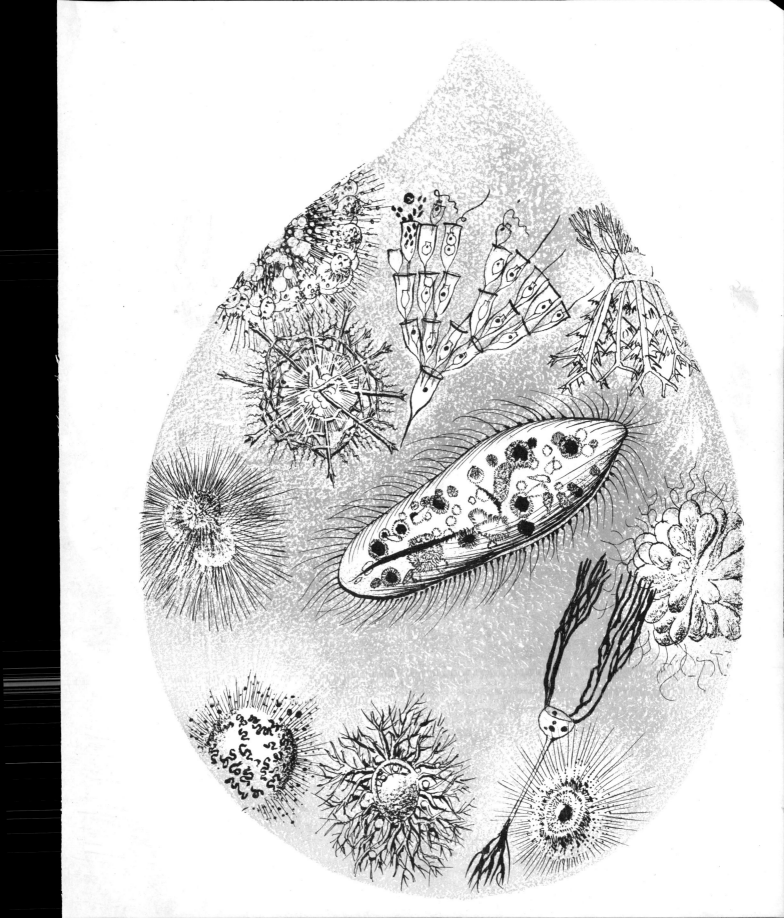

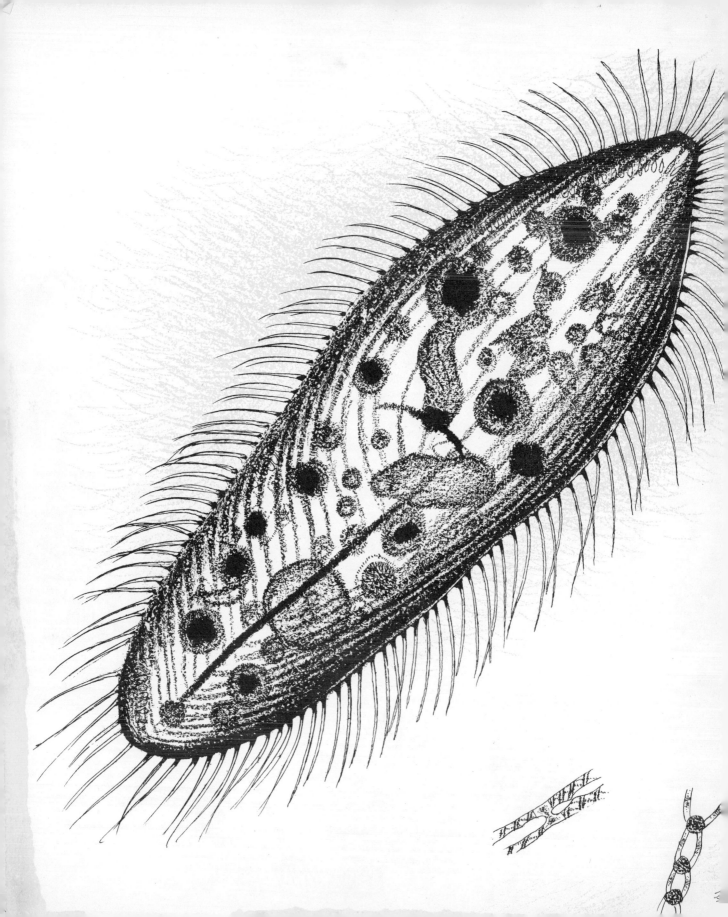

No. Protozoa are tiny animals, but the water plants which protozoa eat are much tinier. These plants, called algae,* are the green grass of the water world. The picture shows what some of the different kinds of algae look like under a powerful microscope. Most algae are so small that you cannot see them even as tiny specks. But millions and millions of tiny algae together make the pale green color of the water in a fish bowl.

Is anything smaller than these algae?

---

*Pronounced *al-jee*.

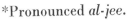

Yes. There are things even smaller than algae—things millions of times smaller. These are the things of which everything and everybody is made. They are called atoms. This is how an atom would look next to one of the tiniest algae.

Imagine how small atoms are. Your hand is made of more atoms than there are leaves on all the trees, fishes in all the seas, people in all the world.

Can anything possibly be smaller than an atom?

Yes. Each atom is made of things that are smaller still. These things are called electrons, protons, and neutrons. No one has ever seen them clearly, but we think they look like this.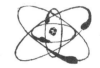

You can't see them even with the most powerful microscope. But in every flash of lightning that rips across the sky you see millions, and billions, and trillions of electrons streaking from one cloud to another or from a cloud to the earth.

Electrons, protons, neutrons— these are the smallest things we know in all the world.

So many things smaller and smaller. So many things bigger and still bigger. Where do you belong?

You belong right in the middle, between an electron and a star.

A star is many, many times bigger than you are. But you are just about as many, many times bigger than an electron.

You are just the right size.

How Big And How Small

THE BIG THINGS

You are about four feet tall.

An elephant is about eleven feet tall.

A very tall oak tree is about 140 feet tall.

The tallest building in the world, the Empire State Building, is 1250 feet, or about a quarter of a mile, high.

The tallest mountain in the world, Mt. Everest, is over 29,000 feet, or about five and a half miles high.

The moon is about 2000 miles in diameter (measuring from one side through the middle to the other side).

The earth is about 8000 miles in diameter (from the North Pole to the South Pole through the center).

The sun is about 860,000 miles in diameter.

Some stars are more than 400 times bigger than the sun.

THE SMALL THINGS

You are about four feet tall.

Puppies come in many sizes, but the one in this book is about one foot tall.

A mouse is about four inches long from the tip of his nose to the end of his tail.

Fifteen ordinary fleas lined up in a row would measure one inch.

There are many sizes of mites, but seventy-five of the smaller kind in a row would measure one inch.

Three hundred medium-sized protozoa in a line would measure one inch.

A thousand medium-sized algae side by side would measure one inch.

Some atoms are much bigger than others, but one hundred million of the biggest atoms in a row would measure one inch.

Electrons, protons, and neutrons are about a million times smaller than atoms.